NEW YORK IN FOCUS

And because no matter who you are, if you believe in yourself and your dream, **New York** will always be the place for you. .

k City Transit

In **New York** it seems like there's no Monday or Saturday or Sunday.

CPSIA information can be obtained
at www.ICGtesting.com
Printed in the USA
BVHW022000150419
545554BV00027B/793/P